Beauty

Find One Beautiful Thing Every Day and Take a Photo of It

CHRISTINA M WILSON

DEDICATION

Lovingly dedicated to all my family.

I believe there is a magnet in all of us which draws us toward one another.

Your assignment is to find

one beautiful thing

every day

and take a photo of it.

(The p o e m s are extra.)

Here are some results.

Stopping by Flowers on a Preschool Morning

Little girl stops by amazing flowers

"I love these flowers" she says

gramma loves these flowers too

and you are the prettiest of all

Apples on a Wet Day

unkempt abundance

joy and decadence mixed

life just beginning

falling again

visual splendor

hurrying by

shuttered—

Silly Raindrop

caught by Sky

Simple Pleasures in the Slow Lane

Before the Caregivers Arrive

Beauty is …

a 2 hour coffee driven conversation

with my Sweetie

at McDonald's

It's a weekly thing

plain and simple

no excuses needed

Sister Greets Sister

Just joy

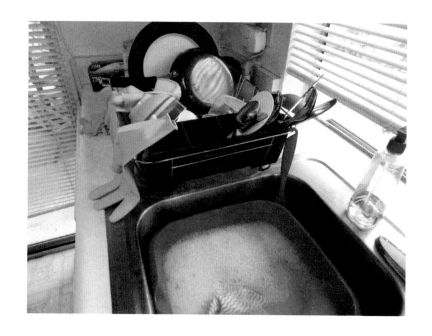

Hand Washed Dishes

It's been tough the last few days

battling emotions

so they don't take hold of me

to rule and ruin me

at least I got those dishes washed

a cleaned up sink always cheers me

Celebration

Creamy blossom in the sky

heaven decreed light show celebrates

Grandbaby's birth

God's way of showing me

he hears and knows my heart's joy

confirms

receives

my worship gladly

14

Ain't Done Lovin' the Rain

I think we need
to make the rain our friend
silvery wet stuff
falling from the sky
like adding smudge and blur or noise and multiply
so many things go wrong
without it–brown trees
all over town
they hack and chop
and cart away
they'll never come back
brown grass and shriveled leaves
a dullish shade of green with gray–
but mostly
rain draws me upward
to consider and ask
what is going on here?
why choose wetness from the sky?
earth inside her mother's womb
reborn before our very eyes
God you are amazing

Even at a Mall

Spring comes early in Southern Cal

shooting stars,

pear blossoms

freely bloom

even a shopping center

can feel expansive

like you're on an excursion

into nature

on a Sunday afternoon

Beautiful Bible Study Ladies

Beautiful ladies dear friends

you who keep me accountable

pushing forward in John's gospel

finished

all the way to the end

thank-you

for your faithfulness

your ability to listen

with hearts open wide

your great encouragement

all the way to the end

finished

thank-you

I love you

dear Bible study friends

Prayer Warriors

Those daffodils
they won't give up
prayer warriors
of the spring
they blare their horns
and shout loudly
when no other
flowers abound
thank you daffodils
for reminding me
to keep my eyes ahead
to not take no
for an answer
The thermometer
and cloudy skies
discourage
when long times have passed
but your bright countenances
keep prayer and hope alive

Mellow Sunday

Spring has sprung finally in Seattle

one month ago just rain

and buds waiting to blossom

they're full now picture perfect

and the warm sun draws cats and people

out of doors to barbecue

and savor the richness of being

family together

Seattle Western Sunny Side Up

sunny day

throughout the sum

of all the daylight hours

Seattle's western sandwich

puts gladness in the bank

early morning walkers

out to catch a brew

joggers strollers

cyclists

children young adults

laughing shouting

having fun

some playing

with their dogs

rain behind and rain ahead

this day will see us through

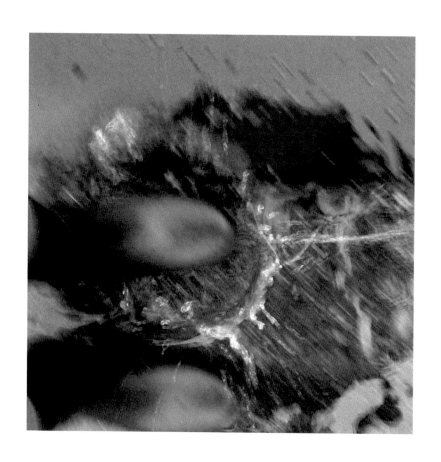

Quiet Day Indoors

Taxes! I did the taxes

had to get them done

my March/April schedule

doesn't allow for taxes

so what should have been

a wonderful exciting day

out in the rain

turned into

sitting at home distracted

jumping up every half hour

to look out the window

hearing the wind the falling rain

the only thing

that salvaged my day

with beauty

is this photo

I took on my silly cell phone

early in the morning

I really like it

such a picture makes me glad

Granddaughter's Work Station

My granddaughter's workstation

reveals who she is

yet not what she will be

so many opportunities

so many directions

it seems clear

for now

maybe not later

that she likes to paint

and the colors blue

purple and green

three years old

spokes of a wheel

all pointing outward

Welding

Learning to weld

practice a bit

willing to try anything with her hands

always active never still

planting weeding sorting chopping cooking

cutting painting this and that

art craft life combined

visible sparks excite

32

Friend in a Ditch

Beauty is … the friend
who crouches
in a cold, wet ditch
listening for the leak
that still plagues
my main water line
He knows nothing about buying
a romantic gift
nor even one that's original
except maybe
the time he bought me
the unabridged dictionary
for my birthday
we weren't getting along by then
I still use it all the time
the gardening tools for Christmas
I could have done without those
but enough
you get the idea
now
it's simple chocolate
albeit the best in town
This is the guy
who thoroughly enjoys McDonald's
for Thursday breakfast
then spends the next four hours
looking for that baffling leak
gift is action
that benefits
only me not him
Should I still be pushing for changes
or simply take him as he is?

Still Friends

Four decades later

our children all grown

and we are still friends

today we spoke openly

about how stubborn each of us is

admitted our fault

and promised to do better

so as not to butt heads

as much as we usually do

winning doesn't matter that much anymore

it's more about caring for the other

Pastel Day

Almond petals

like snow blossoms

perch upon the boughs

break the monotony

of straight highways

and seemingly

endless miles

Cherry Blossoms

wet shivery day

exposure set high

focus softened

edges blended

unlike rain

and cold air

sharp silhouettes

against pink petals

image created

cherry blossoms

memory to hang

keep forever

while thoughts of cold

dim and fade

Red Maple

Came home from being away awhile

winter had turned to spring

clouds to sun

wet to dry

cool to warm

so surprised and pleased

in this morning's soft light

to see my old friend

the red maple

in glorious form

so much better than last year

this third year in a potting tub

so I can roll it

here and there

seeking to protect it

by providing shade

that barely exists

on my small patio yard

Hello!

What a wonderful greeting!

should I call this a sign?

Warm Fire Chillish Evening

Feeling just sick enough
with a strongish aching in the back
and a craving for rest
to justify canceling
the evening's social activity
square dancing
and the air being chillish
it seemed a good opportunity
to sit warmly by the fire
continue reading this book
the best book I've run into
after years of searching
on my favorite topic
the hot tea was good
the water cool and refreshing
the book great
but mainly it was the fire
sput-sput-sputtering warm flames
that captured me
and healed my soul
sometimes sickness
is a good thing

First Ice Cream

we shared an ice cream cone today

from Millie's ice cream shop

we will never forget the walk in the rain

and the sprinkles on the top

the little girl singing all the way home

skipping and hopping down the block

When Help Comes

When help comes it's a beautiful thing

immediate help

timely help

not having-been-nagged-into-it help

willing help

cheerful help

capable help

to fix what has long been broken

it seems I only needed to ask

and that's the part that needs the most help

thank you dear sweet kind Helper

double entendre intended

Dragon Fruit

Hylocereus undatus
exotic fruit
from an exotic land
surely it must be exotic
because I am a tourist here
and I don't see this fruit back home …
riding the bus
to see where it goes
riding back again
hopping off to visit awhile
not knowing what we'll find
maybe the best caf
I've ever tasted
maybe an out of this world
whole wheat
blueberry muffin
juicy not too sweet
or perhaps the flakiest
baklava
I've ever laid eyes on
(we gave it as a gift)
maybe we'll find this exotic fruit
called dragon

Developmental Stages

Little girl in tutu

tumbling on the floor

as chaotic as your petticoats

who will you grow to be?

sometimes yes sometimes no

never in-between

setting out your boundaries

for all the world to see

I as your gramma

just want to squeeze you tight

my days are few yours are many

independence is your right

when I wait with patience

give you all your space

you come around with gentleness

to give a warm embrace

My Daughter

Happy Birthday dear daughter

who cooked her own

birthday brunch

to share

with all of us

for yours is the talent

servant's heart

so easily pleased

by pleasing others

you smooth the way

for all of us

to enjoy

and find delight

I appreciate you

and I love you very much

People Helping People

Everyone is good at something

I never met anyone good at nothing

when all the somethings combine

that's some good

Rescued

Stranded without my car keys

a bagful of heavy canned goods

and fresh meat

Dear friend

who had canceled our weekly breakfast

because I was coughing

and he didn't want to catch it

arrived in less than twenty minutes

to carry me home and back

with my spare set

now that's a beautiful sight for sick eyes

Backyard

My friends' backyard
is the prettiest backyard
I have ever seen
Mike is a landscape gardener
and now that I mention it
how strange …
every time I visit
he is sitting back relaxing
yet he alone does all this labor
mostly folk art
no classes no lessons
just a natural love
for beauty and color
finding ceramics, dinnerware
broken pieces of tile
he smashes–creates anew
creatures and birds
architecture and seas.
While growing plants and flowers
is his specialty
talking birds participate
from their safe house just beyond
Mike's a wonder
as is Claudia my friend
who prepares a meal fit for royalty
from their garden just below
what makes these people most special
is their love
for everyone
for me
for you

Roosters Crow in Cold Seattle

silly willy daffodillies

calling out the dawn

impatient buds, frantic

pushing down the barn

"Wake up! Wake up! You sleepy heads!

The business day has dawned.

All the world will pass you by

as you take your final yawn.

Sloppy Blessings

Muddy blessings

sloppy blessings

in the mix of life

growth is not homogenous

nothing in life is

swimming through a pond of pain

is beauty all around

expectational adjustment

grants us peace within